SANCTUAIRE

SANÇTUAIRE

The Traveler's Journals

VOLUME THREE

BY

FREYDIS LOVA

LA RÉPUBLIQUE FRANÇAISE

2024

The Traveler's Journals

TABLE OF CONTENTS

SANCTUARY
(ENGLISH)

/ sæŋk-tʃu-er-i /

noun

1. A place of refuge or safety.

TO THE MAN WITH THE BLUE EYES
AND A DREAM OF SOMETHING MORE—

I HOPE YOU'VE FOUND
WHAT YOU WERE SEARCHING FOR.

What Are The Traveler's Journals?

I've dreamt of traveling the world for as long as I can remember.
When I was little, I had these grand ideas of exploring— of
writing and painting and creating, of meeting the sun and
moon along different coordinate lines as though they were
strangers, but falling in love with them just the same,
if not more.

As life went on, traveling never became more than the dream it
started as. Until, that is, I decided to wake up and embrace the
uncertainty of taking risks.

And so, *The Traveler's Journals* were born.

The Traveler's Journals are a collection of poetry that span the globe.
In each volume, you will discover a series of stories from a
single country— a life briefly lived, surrounded by strangers
and unfamiliar architecture. Of love letters and fantasies, of
histories and what-ifs that became memories instead of staying
daydreams. *The Traveler's Journals* are chambers of my heart,
written in different dialects and given to you, so that you may
explore the world with me.

Welcome, wildflowers, to my journals.
Read them.
Write in them.
Fall in love with life.
Fall in love with strangers.

Stain the pages with tea, or coffee, or rain from wherever you
are in the world. Take them with you to the country they're
dedicated to and fill them with your own thoughts.
In these moments, these words are just as much yours as they
are mine. Let them help guide you through dreamscapes and
across oceans.

With every speck of stardust,

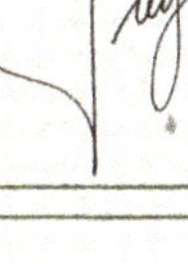

Poems

Blue velvet rises,
pulled to the sides and
beyond the fading chandelier.
I steady my breathing,
gingerly twisting the ends of my shawl
instead of laying my hands
patiently in my lap.

Moments ago, I was half blind,
looking for a contact lens
at the bottom of a bag in a hotel bathroom.
Now I'm here with you,
and we're here with them.

They float among the echoes and ghosts
in the heaviest silence the byzantine night
can stand. But there's more to it— to them.
Surrounding their stage is a spectacle of
viridian and gold, shrouded in pearl luster.

You reach for my hand but pull back
as the orchestra begins to play.

The curtain finishes its ascension.
The shadows stay still as they're illuminated.

This isn't an opera.
This is life.

The show begins.

Lovers behind masks
play with heartstrings,
plucking violins I haven't touched
in twenty years.

I cry as quietly as I can,
trying not to miss a single moment
of their story.

I selfishly wonder if anyone
feels the same way about me.

It's funny, in an ironic sort of way.
I never liked *Romeo and Juliet.*
I got tired of reading it every year for school.
But here I am, seated in the center of an opera house,
next to you in the shrouds of darkness
at your invitation, and I can't think of you.
I'm too busy breaking over a love story
I've spent the latter part of my life being angry at.

Is this what they mean by
love is madness?

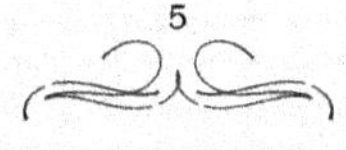

He lays her down in a boat of flowers.

He kisses her lips.

Her neck.

Stomach.

Thighs.

She kisses his tears.

Pink lips taste the sweetest
when they're feeding you lies.

She says, *Je vous aime.*

Her lips stain his red.

Don't let her go, you fool.

This staircase to nowhere
leads to hell. An inferno of infatuation,
of lust and loss of life.
Love has no place here.
That's how I knew she would die
before her first act ended.

Now that she's breathing
death through living lungs,
I can't look away.

A boat for a bed,
a burial for a wedding.
Flowers decay before they bloom
in this twisted labyrinth
turning in place— a chained ballerina
performing for spirits
of priests and parents.

She sings of love and pain.
I sing no more.
If I were to sing of you,
would my notes make those around me
cry just the same?
The only melody they'll get from me
are the letters I'll burn
in a dead fire, no longer in my heart.

Her song will haunt these halls
well beyond the days when
a new story has taken its place
on a stage with new strangers.

Romeo drinks the poison.
I expect him to fall— to slowly
sink to his knees in an all too eager
proposal to Death. Instead, he stands.
He sings. And Juliet wakes.

It's only when he's in her arms
that he lets himself collapse.

Be strong for love.

Sometimes, being strong
means showing weakness.
I watch on through scared tears.

She sings, but he doesn't hear her.
She cries, but he doesn't see her.
He reaches a hand to her face
and their melodies clash
in a symphony of disasters.

His final breath draws on
for four more measures,
and then four more.

He takes ten minutes to die.

Juliet lets go long before then.

He stole her life
and her death.

Juliet loses Romeo.
Everyone loses Juliet.

This midnight matinee menagerie
is a dance I can't breathe through.

There's a never-ending standing ovation.
My body is pulled this way and that
by the applause— a tide being pushed
through the performers.
I hardly see you through the salt-staining streaks
rolling down my cheeks, ruining my mascara.
I smile at their bitter sting and burn my hands
as they clap for every actor, every musician,
every cell that carried life into this production.

I welcome the heartbreak along with the cliché.

Both feel safe here.

Le rideau se ferme
et s'écrase sur la scène.

Tu t'écrases en moi.

The curtain closes,
crashing down on the stage.

You crash into me.

He walks me through a little market
overrun with old men and middle-aged ladies
with pipes hanging out of scowls
and black handbags bumping into roses.
The roads leave little room for the footfall
of visitors trying to navigate this new world of noise.

We're halfway to the hotel
when it starts to rain.
It's a light drizzle at first.
It poses no real danger.
But then the merchants
begin to pack up their stalls,
and in mere moments,
the only light we see is
the soft smudges of street lamps
and the specks of orange
ends of cigarette butts as they
extinguish themselves behind
closing tent flaps and
an asphalt atmosphere.

Paris cries for the loss of the sun.
I fade into her as I cry for the loss of Paris.
Together, we would have cried for the loss of love
if one wouldn't come back to live another day.

We forego turning right as the storm carries on.
He carries my curiosity down a side street,
insisting he knows where he is.

I follow him blindly, trusting
that he can see better than I can
in the rain, beneath the white shirt,
held high in surrender to the weather.

If I listen closely, I can hear the city
whispering directions through the echoes
of wing tips and wedge heels
splashing through flooding streets.

We find sanctuary in a little crêpe shop
on the corner of Who-Knows-Where
and Someplace North. It's across from a cat café.

We add it to our list of side quests.

It's nearly time to leave again
when we get back to the hotel.
The rain was kind enough to
grant us passage after soaking our bones.
I fix my makeup in the lobby bathroom.
He runs upstairs and smooths out his hair.

It's a shame–

I think his curls are cute.

And then I see them,
and it doesn't matter
that I'm drenched and freezing,
because the lobby is filling with the warmth
of my favorite Tennessee sunflowers.

We're a disaster of damp dresses and daydreams,
clinging to each other as the sunset breaks through
just in time to wish us a first goodnight.

And what a good night it is—

Our short walk to dinner
is over a mile of winding streets,
dodging cars, and carefully mapping
out the way back so we won't have to
think as hard after the wine.
The car horns blast a final time
before the roads clear out, leaving us
to a night of blistered feet and memories.

Huddled beneath an awning,
we talk about favorite movies.

He hasn't seen any of mine.

He asks me to make a list.

She smiles across the table from me—
the sweet soul I met at the airport.
We passed each other so many times
trying to find our way.
And then we paused, caught our breath,
and laughed. And how sweet it was,
to laugh and no longer be alone.

She reminds me of a young poet I met in Italy—
Kaitlyn.
Shy, caring, and kind eyes filled with hope.
I know that she's a sunflower at heart,
but here, she is pure starlight.

After hours have passed
and we've stumbled back—
tired, and full, and feet aching—
we fall into a blissful daze
of chocolate and strawberry,
red wine and rain.

He sees me fumbling with the clasp of my necklace
over a cup of coffee and a plate of eggs and sausage.
The morning has been kind in its victory,
and gifts the defeated souls tea and chocolate croissants
in return for a restless night behind us and a day of walking ahead.

I accept my fate, slip my necklace into my bag, and join him.

I will never say no to butter and chocolate.

I'm a firm believer that poets
share the same mind and heart,
the same way cats all share
the same brain cell.

We may speak different languages
and call different doors home,
but everyone at our table is wrapping
tiny pastries in napkins and sneaking them
into their bags for our later adventures.

Il me le demande avec ses yeux.

Cela ne devrait pas me prendre au dépourvu—

il a toujours été un gentleman—

mais pour une raison quelconque, c'est le cas.

Peut-être parce que je ne m'y attendais pas.

Ses yeux sont une langue

que je ne parle qu'une fois par an,

mais je la comprendrai toujours

aussi clairement que ma langue maternelle.

Je lui donne la chaîne en argent

et j'écarte mes cheveux

tandis qu'il se positionne derrière moi.

Il a la gentillesse de faire attention

de ne pas effleurer mon cou avec ses doigts.

He asks me with his eyes.
It shouldn't catch me off guard—
he's always been a gentleman—
but for some reason, it does.
Maybe because I wasn't expecting it.
His eyes are a language
I speak but once a year,
yet will always understand
as clearly as my mother tongue.

I hand him the silver chain
and pull my hair out of the way
as he positions himself behind me.

He's kind enough to be careful
not to brush his fingers against my neck.

I would like to know how many ways
exist to say, *I love you.*

Le Mur Des J'e T'aime says, *311.*
The locks on the fences say, *endless.*

There's a moment
as I'm walking
through the scattered light
speckling the letters,
hieroglyphs, and heartbreak,
that I think of adding a lock
for us. For *you*.
But my heart and brain know better.

I find the words in Norwegian instead.

Jeg elsker deg.

I find the hand speaking sign
and hold mine up to mirror it
for good measure.
And for Jacob.

That's the part about love
that no one tells you about.
The ending part.
The sudden stop that leaves
your feelings scattered
as you're trying to figure out
how you're still moving.
How something so linear
is now branching off
in a million directions.

How, when the love doesn't die,
but you know you have to put yourself first,
everything feels so far away
but you feel so claustrophobic.

How hard it is to not say, *I love you,*
when both of you still do,
because for right now,
you need to love yourself more.

My heart is a compass
whose strings are woven
with roses and thorns
and directions to the next destination.

His heartbeat matches the coordinates.

Maybe Paris is the place you go
when your heart needs to rest
after piecing itself back together.

How many times can a poet write *I*?
How many times can we selfishly center
our words around ourselves?
How many times can we string you along
through our lives, our happiness, our pain?

Poets love pain best.
He's our closest friend.
We make love to shadows
and bloom in cemeteries,
watered with the tears we shed for others—
for those who don't know the end yet.

Our ends so very often
meet us in the middle of the story.
So how many times?
I want to know the answer.

But right now, I want to know you more.

Every road, every river, every piece of art
that embellishes your streets.
I want to meet you on a bridge
and see how we begin—
this new, temporary life.

I want to know why
Vincent and Claude loved you so—
if I can love you just as much.

Please, don't let us be strangers anymore.

The mountain is tall
and our legs are weary.
But this is an adventure,
and so we step on.

Je t'aime?

I don't know yet.

It's never-ending, but I don't mind.
Here, birds fly still, cemented in stone.
They watch us with their unmoving eyes,
guarding something from us strangers.
Or maybe from the flowers
that grow wild and wide
across fences and gates, ivy covering houses,
peonies and lavender bursting with secrets.

How I wish I were a wildflower.

Maybe then I would know better.

We're nearly there.
The quietness of this place
suddenly breaks.

He's the old man of Montmarte,
sitting on the corner with an accordion.

La Vie en Rose.

I find a euro in my wallet
and drop it in his cup.

The cat atop the instrument lifts his head
as if to thank me.
I take out another euro.

I can't thank one and not the other.

I stand there for a few more songs.
The cat sways his tail and tilts his head,
content with nestling down on the other end
of the accordion. His purrs are barely audible
above the hum of keys, keeping time.
He closes his eyes and smiles,
ears tilted back. His owner smiles down at him.

I think he plays more for the cat than the people.

I step away as the crowd grows.
The music begins to fade,
blending with voices of artists.
The square is bustling with life
on canvases. I fall in love
with a painting of sunflowers.

Somewhere between the deep green and gold,
I see them— my familiar faces.
There's thirteen of them, laying imperfectly
in acrylic in front of ivory, pale blue,
and every other color
of a muted, Florence sky.

I know these flowers are meant to be French,
but even still, I can't help but think
that somehow the artist and I have
a thread connecting our histories—

all of our sunflowers.

The artist in question is nowhere to be found.

I wait for five minutes before moving on.

I regret not going back and buying it.

Cachée dans les collines,
je suis avalée par la fumée
de cigarette et la poussière de charbon de bois.
Mes poumons s'arrêtent de bouger,
et je suis jetée contre du papier de coton.
Mon esprit traverse des flaques d'eau
en attendant le pigment, pendant que les gens me dépassent
comme des coups de pinceau,
me guidant dans toutes les directions.

Je veux peindre à nouveau,
mais pour l'instant,
je serai heureuse dans cette scène
éclaboussée d'aquarelles.

Hidden in the hills,
I am swallowed by smoke
from cigarettes and charcoal dust.
My lungs stop moving,
and I am thrown against cotton paper.
My mind runs in the puddles of water
waiting for pigment, people passing me
over like brush strokes,
guiding me every which way.

I want to paint again,
but for right now,
I will be happy in this scene,
splashed in watercolors.

I ease my way out of the painting
and am immediately pulled back to you.
We wander the square, watch new friends
have their portraits done and strangers stand
in line for coffee and crêpes. We explore the roads
around it. The old man of Montmarte and his cat
are gone. We hide in the shadows of an alleyway.

Every inch of wall and ceiling
are covered in notes left by visitors.
You said you found this place
a few days ago and wanted to share it with us.
Our little group forms again
and we duck down to enter in
through the low doorway.

Crammed in a corner, I look around
and wonder which of my words
might be important enough to leave behind.

None of us leave our mark.

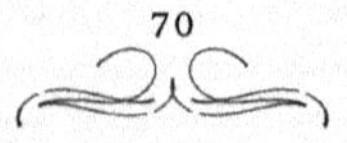

How can a heart that is so full
of words to share,
love to give, and dreams to live,
so often be left speechless,
beating against thinning air,
struggling to communicate?

I fear that if you took my pulse,
fingers beneath my jaw or hand on my chest,
the stuttering of my tongue-tied chambers
wouldn't make the slightest bit of sense.

Is this how art is supposed to make you feel?

Burn my heart beneath the sun.
Make me a martyr at the top of the mountain.
After climbing every step,
after twisting and turning and struggling to speak,
I see her in the distance.

The little girl in me is silent.
She dreamt of you for so long,
and then, one day, stopped.
This trip is for her.
Now, her heart is awake again.

The Eiffel Tower stands miles away.
Soon, I'll look up instead of out.

We sit on a stone bench.

Our teacher tells us about ekphrastic poetry.

I feel less silly for talking to paintings.

They say to have courage,
but what if that's not what I need?
What if this heart
was always meant to be broken?
To be imperfect and cracked?
Missing pieces, stolen, tired,
on display for a conglomerate of people?

I sit there, still as the seat beneath me.
I don't need courage—
not right now.
I need to give myself a little grace
and remember that not every work of art
is complete.

But that doesn't make it any less beautiful.

Sometimes,
the hardest part
about having a loving heart
is not having enough of it
to love yourself.

Would you kiss me if I let you?
Berry sweet with honey,
we jump from shadow to shadow
on this sunburnt street that lines the river.

The mist is cool, the water, enough.

How wonderful that must be.

To be enough.

It's okay to be selfish with me.

We're laughing, talking, forgetting, getting lost.
The church is grand, but we pay it no mind.
We have tote bags filled with art and baguettes,
blisters between our toes, and dreams that bind us.
How could we possibly sit still any longer?

There are birds and bodies everywhere—
painted in bright colors and plastered on
the sides of buildings. A snake coils
around a doorway. I run my fingertips
over him, half expecting to feel the ridges
of scales. The wall is smooth. I am still amazed.

He walks through the wall
and into my memory.
His hand is stretched out,
either in movement
or a silent plea for help.
I reach my hand to his
but do not take it.

I sometimes wonder
what would have happened
if I did.

I'm descending the mountain
by way of lavender fields.
The air tastes like honey.
I smile and think of you,
relieved that, even though it hurts,
there's a peace that lays with it
between the flowers, beneath the sun.

My burial and rebirth
were held at the same time.
It made the invitations easy—
one location, one date, one RSVP.
And even still, I was
the only one to attend.
And even still, the foxgloves
grew above my crown
and below my roots.

I become a new person
every time I visit a new country.

This time, I'm yours.

Belonging to a place
is far more freeing
than belonging to
a longing heart.

There's a baby pink Volkswagen Beetle
on the side of the road.
I half expect subtitles reading,
Sacré- Cœur, 1970,
to appear in the air in front of me.

No one stands beside it.
The stone chateau is dark.
The day is young, and I
can hear a song stirring in the air.

Je regarde l'âme
avec des bagues à chaque doigt
et le sac plein de livres.

Elle nous guide
dans la scène d'ouverture
d'un nouveau film classique.

I look over at the soul
with rings on every finger
and the bag full of books.

She leads us on
into the opening scene
of a new, classic film.

On to a shrine.
A tomb.
A display, captured behind ropes
and mounted on pedestals.
It's another labyrinth,
and I feel my heart awaken
at the chance of meeting them.

I know better than to run
through this maze. I don't want
to miss anything. Anyone.
I've waited years to meet them.
They're not expecting me,
nor will they remember me,
but I'll remember them.

That's how it usually works with love.
At least with lovers.
One heart beats steadily,
another breaks, and both awaken.

My dear, darling one,
I recognize that look in your eyes.
An endless darkness has been broken
by breath and embrace.
He is haloed in all things light—
this savior of yours, so tenderly
leaning over you as if to shield you
from all things wicked except himself.
To shield you from us.
But you don't notice us.
You only see him.
And as you reach up to pull him back down
into another kiss, my heart breaks
because everyone knows your fate but you.

Where is she?
Where is the rest of her?
Tell me what you've done.
Where are her arms?
How can she hold tight
to hope and love without them?
How can she wipe away tears
without her hands?
How can she smile, or sing,
or see how breathtaking the dawn is
without her head?
And what of her thoughts
that may have changed the world?
They have silenced her in word and action.

Time is no less cruel to woman than
the men who stand around her
in prestine condition.

You had her entire life to immortalize,
and yet you chose her death.
Chose the moment she fell,
the moment she crumbled
beneath the brink. That's your way,
though, isn't it, Eugène?
To see a woman's weakness
as a beautiful tragedy
instead of accepting their strength?
You make the river rise,
the waves appear far taller than
they really are. You kiss us
until we can't breathe
and laugh as we gasp for air.
You could have chosen any instance
of happiness. Instead, you have made it
so history will always know how she left us
without telling us whose fault it was.
They will see her as beautiful but certifiable.
The women will stand silently
and send a prayer back in time
in hopes that somewhere, somehow,
the pages will change to tell the story
of a woman who left without leaving the earth.

He's been standing there for an hour now.
I've seen him every time I've wandered
through the marble halls, trying to find
my way to the next room.
The same spot. The same position.
I sit in the shadowed cut out on
the other side of the corridor.
He's sketching the angels in the case.
Gods look down on him
and he tilts his sketchpad to show them.
Their faces, though stone, look pleased.
I wonder if he knows that
he is just as much a masterpiece
as the small statues in the glass cage.

The old man closes his book,
sighs, and looks back at the angels.
As the pages fall forward,
I can see that they're all filled
with the same sad face and wings.
With her hands over her heart,
she watches him leave again and again.

She can't go with him.

He fiddles with his wedding band.
Centuries before he was even a thought,
someone sculpted his wife
so that even when Fate tore them apart,
they could still somehow be together.

She bumped into him while taking a step back.
If he had been a second earlier,
or a heartbeat later, it would have never happened.
They mumble apologies, cheeks flushing
and eyes darting anywhere but to each other.
Then they pause, and the people passing by
become extra statues, clustered in the open space.

Venus smiles down on them.
They leave the room together.

And then there's the elderly couple,
sitting on the bench and watching
generations pass by. They hold hands
and he squeezes hers as if to say,
Do you remember when that was us?

She lets her wrinkles shine—
a testament to every happy day with him.
She kisses his cheek and he blushes—
a schoolboy at heart, still very much
in love with his only sweetheart.

Sometimes I think that
my favorite part of going to a museum
isn't to look at the art,
but to watch people fall in love.

There's a line for *Mona Lisa*
that spans four hours long.
I send her a coy smile
as I pass, remembering
our secret encounter in Norway.

Kissing you feels like drowning
beneath Monet's water lilies.

I have Vincent Van Gogh's nose—
long, crooked, and rigid.
I contour it with swirls and stars,
trying so desperately
to match the pattern each day.

He kisses the bridge
and calls me beautiful.

I wonder what my mania will be.

Somewhere in Paris,
a candle is lit in someone's memory.

Somewhere in Paris,
someone is praying for love.

Somewhere in Paris,
church bells echo through empty alleyways.

Somewhere in Paris,
I leave our forever in a graveyard.

I will paint myself a masterpiece
with my words and woes,
and they will cover up my scars
so that one day, no man will
look upon me and only see me
drowning in my weakest moment.

A strand of pearls,
bridal white for a single sinner.
A tube of lipstick, forever red.
A green satin bow with a silver clasp.
Letters written in lingerie.

What is this country doing to me?

Should we go out and join them?

No. Let's go to bed.
Our future selves will thank us in the morning.

Neither of us sleep,
a floor between our heads.

Les rêves ne viennent pas en dormant ici.
Ils viennent quand on est bien éveillé
allongé, agité, enveloppé dans les couvertures
tricotées de ce qui pourrait être et peut-être.

Dreams don't come in sleep here.
They come when you're wide awake,
laying restless, wrapped in blankets
knit of *what-could-be* and *maybe*.

Coffee wakes me before the sun.
He's the first to rise,
already out and about and exploring
before the day spreads over the fields.
I spread myself over the bed and stretch,
wondering if I should go back to sleep.
Against my better judgement,
I get up, get ready, and go down the stairs.

He walks up to me before I can notice him.
He holds out his hands, expectantly.
I hand him my necklace.
His fingers linger.

My morning is engulfed with flowers.
Rich yellows and purples, bursts of
bright colors surrounding me.
It smells of summer and hope and
perfume I wore all too long ago.
It brings me back to the days
before I found my voice, my name,
myself. I think of the women at the museum—
cold, incomplete, and trapped in marble.

Is this how they felt before *after?*

The hardest part
about trying to write
in a city of voices
is trying to keep your own.

Poetry is all around me.
It's in the gardens, the songs,
the silence. It's in the children's laughter
and the lovers' quarrel.

Love isn't the only thing in the air.

How is it that this place can feel so empty?
The streets, the markets, the parks—
I would have thought they would be
swarmed with people. But somehow,
they're just as alive as the ghosts.
The painters at Montmare,
the man with the accordion and the cat,
the vendors by the opera house—
they leave their mark in my mind
and in my journal, and then disappear.

I'm scared to write about you,
worried you'll do the same.

But life is worth taking risks.

I skip the cobblestones along the river,
tiptoes dancing as I take note of
fruit baskets and flower arrangements.
Last summer, I wrote about a table
in the solarium of a little hotel's sun room
in a secluded Italian town.

I wonder if I can do that here—
to be so frivolous with my words
in a country that's so serious.

Words, it would seem, follow me everywhere.
They're written on statues, vandalizing walls
in chalk and neon paints, stuck onto windows,
and yelled across the street in little messages
meant for strangers. I find myself growing more silent
each day, over each village and town line,
and lose myself in a wonderful daydream
where my voice doesn't feel so tired.

My voice feels small.
My body feels big.
Hello, Dysmorphia—
I didn't think you had a passport.

I take pictures of globes,
of girls posing by shop signs,
of a woman on a bike in front of
an ivy-covered café.

It takes me days to work up the courage
to ask someone to take a picture of me.

I never photograph well.
I always hold my head too high or too low,
forcing a smile too wide for my face.
Always overthinking.
That's how I spent the majority of my life, though—
overthinking.
Making sure I fit into the mold others made for me.

The mold may be broken,
but the thoughts still linger.

Even still, I find more joy in
capturing the moment for others.

Maybe one day I'll have my picture taken
and feel content with how I look.
No stroke eye, no lopsided grin—
a relaxed face. Something natural.
Something that feels happy.

We come to a church
and I ask a god I haven't spoken to in years
to forgive me for my vanity.

She's setting up a vintage camera,
plaid dress swishing around her legs
as she dances around the stand.
I hear others talking about her.
She's often found here, capturing memories.
She doesn't ask for much— donate what you can.

She finishes her dance and looks through the lens,
then smiles, satisfied with what she's accomplished.
I watch and wait. When no one goes up to her,
he stands and leads me over.

She greets us kindly
and thanks us when
we drop a few euro
into her collection box.

Then she poses us
in front of Notre Dame,
telling us where to stand,
what to do with our arms,
where to look. We do our best.

She takes one picture,
then tells us to pose for another.
She asks us to look at each other.
We only last a second before we break
eye contact and laugh, whole-hearted and light.

She takes a second picture.
Both are printed on sheets that look like
newspapers— our photos on the front page.

He keeps the one of us laughing.

Across the bridge is a book store.
This is just as dangerous as the gelato shop.
The only thing keeping me from filling my arms
with new stories is the lack of room in my suitcase.

La chose la plus imprudente
que j'ai jamais faite
a été de donner un livre à quelqu'un
sans savoir
de quoi parlait l'histoire.

THE MOST RECKLESS THING
I'VE EVER DONE
WAS GIVE SOMEONE A BOOK
WITHOUT KNOWING
WHAT THE STORY WAS ABOUT.

I buy a copy of *The Hunchback of Notre Dame*.
It's in French and has a map of Paris
serving as its cover, and will be
a beautiful reminder of my time here.

I fold the picture from earlier in half
and tuck it between two random pages.
A one-way metro pass, the opera ticket,
and a scrap of poem join it.
It's a photo album of us,
wandering the lost paths,
searching for something more.

This place is a church itself—
statues formed of sonnets,
saints and sinners alike, gathered
to pay tithes and offerings.
We read from the same scriptures,
sing praise of our saviors,
share books with strangers.
Leather-bound and paperback press
together in windows— stained glass
our Sun can't shine through.

This is the place where poets come to worship.

Today is a day for church.
It isn't a Sunday,
there isn't any set structure,
nor is there a sermon or priest.
Yet here we are,
slowly piling into another
house for Catholic hearts.
She's grand, and her marble is dark.
I try to imagine what she looked like
when she was new, light, bright,
and hope was an abundant dream to cling to.

I leave a simple donation
in a wooden box, tucked away
in the corner behind grand columns,
out of sight of the saints.

I tip toe over to the next space,
terrified that if I make the slightest sound,
it will echo into eternity, and they'll know I'm here.

I light candles for the dead.
For Joe. For Fran. For Richard.
Humble little tea lights
stacked up along an iron ivy stem.
I lose myself in their flames—
in their memories—
as they settle down.
I make sure the candles face the alter.
I think they would have liked that.

Despite the offerings,
despite the towering windows,
there is little light here.
Little warmth.
I wrap my arms around me
and remind myself that
I'm here for them—
those I've lost,
and the little girl who used to believe.

He doesn't practice, but he lights a candle anyway.
Ash sizzles beneath little, open fires.
Coins clink in a box. The bell strikes twice.
He's here for them, too.

The chill leaves with the side door opening.
It's too hot now.
I follow the cold out to the alley.

People go to church
for the same reason
they go to bars
in five-star hotels.
It's a funeral for the guilt.
Drown your sorrows in wine,
surround yourself in beauty,
try to feel better.
Repeat your penance until it works.

I find sanctuary
between the ivy walls
among the flowers
and the stray cats.

To them, I'm just another church mouse.
They surround me, but seem surprised
when I greet them as old friends rather than run.
They scatter into the shadows when another soul steps out.

He finds sanctuary in me.

Others find us and sit, lining the stone
at the third toll of the bell. I don't know
which ghost rings it— their faces are still blurs—
but I thank them for bringing me back
out of my mind, out of my memories.

I fear that, one day,
I'll find myself
haunting a church
the way ones from my past
haunt me in life.

A woman tells us about her faith.
I think of Catherine and the conversation
we had at the vineyard last summer.
My heart is happy for those
who hold experiences I don't.

*Hey there, princess, or pirate, or painter, or whoever you are
today in that fantastic mind of yours—*

*It's easier when you pretend, isn't it? You don't have to talk
that way. You just walk through the garden gates of that
beautiful imagination and escape into a world of silence.
There's no way to get hurt there. You just see the world as
something far larger than it is—at least to you right now.*

*I'm going to let you in on a little secret: the world you
imagine is actually far smaller than the world we live in.
But despite its size, it's far easier to explore.*

*You've been dreaming of this moment for so long now, I
know. And here we are. We made it.*

*There's no more dreaming. No more wondering. No more
longing.*

*Part of us gave up on this adventure before it was ever really
a possibility. I'm sorry for that. For letting you down and
extinguishing dreams because of fear and noise.*

*I made you a promise, though, and I kept it. The noise isn't
all that bad. In fact, it's been reawakening the symphonies
you composed in your head when you couldn't sleep when
you were so much smaller. They blend well, the melodies.*

*Now you can dance to them in harmony. You can explore
and wander and just exist in the moment. You don't have to
hide anymore.*

For all of the people who underestimated you, encouraged failure, made you think that this was a pipe dream—for me...for older you, who should have encouraged your differences but let you down instead, worried that your mind would be too much to understand...who hid you away and fit you with your first mask— prove us wrong.

Scrape your knees on the rocks by the Seine. Twirl, and sing, and fall upon the grass. Take out your watercolors and paint the tower.

— a letter to my younger self

That's exactly what she does.
Living in my soul, a figment standing next to me
with an easel and smock, pigtails and a beret,
works in silence.

Tongues poke out of the corners of our mouths.
Eyes squint.
Strangers pass through her.
Our creation comes to life on one canvas.

It's messy, and uneven,
and no where close to a masterpiece,
but it's ours, and that's all that matters.

S'IL Y A JAMAIS UN RÊVE
QU'IL NE FAUT JAMAIS ABANDONNER,
QUE CE SOIT CELUI DE L'ENFANCE.

IF THERE IS EVER A DREAM
YOU SHOULD NEVER GIVE UP ON,
LET IT BE THE ONE YOU HAD AS A CHILD.

We gather on a bridge,
away from the crowds.
The summer air bites us
as the sun slips down,
leaving us in darkness.
We pass the time by reading poems.
The same voices share—
Italian memories, the steps that carried us
to each other, every moment before and after.
It's strange, and I'm tired of hearing my own voice.
I'm tired of hearing my own longing.

She chose which poems
she wanted me to share.
I finish reading them
and close my book,
hoping that someone else
will take the makeshift stage.
A twin flame stands at the front
and bares herself to us,
to the others passing by.
We clap for her when she finishes.
The strangers don't.

Poetry is not unusual here.
It's another way of breathing.
To them, we're just existing
through another form of art.

When we run out of words
and scatter along the walk,
our teacher finds me.
She's more soul-sister now.
She asks me what I'm working on.

Besides this book?

She nods.
I open the notes app in my phone
and begin to read.
Every time I finish a poem,
she asks for another.

By the time I'm at the bottom of the page,
she's heard the first fifty poems
of a stand-alone collection
I'm too scared to publish.

And then it happens—
the tower lights up.
She's gorgeous, shimmering
against an indigo midnight.
The scene takes me back to the opera house.
Back to the curtains.
We somehow keep finding our way
back to the city.
I wonder if this curtain is the finale
or merely an intermission.

This sanctuary is different
than the others we've taken
shelter in. It's open, and exposed,
and yet we still feel safe without any walls.

I catch your eye and smile.
A new friend asks me
to take her picture with the tower.
Both of them look radiant.

Hold my waist
and dip me down.
Kiss me as the tower steals the stars.

My lover tastes like watered-down wine
and cigarettes. Or maybe just the wine,
and the cigarettes are from the midnight air,
ash falling in front of twinkling lights.
Except we aren't standing in front of the tower,
and it's seven in the morning.

So why doesn't he taste like coffee and pain au chocolate?

I kiss him again, hoping to find an answer.

It's so quiet outside of the city.
So few people, so few ghosts.
A mist rolls over the countryside,
shadowing the stone and grass
between the buildings.
The air is lighter, lifting our lungs
to whispered songs.
We walk, we look, we write.
Poetry is a memory keeper,
and we are her caretakers.

A raven splashes in a puddle,
wings spread and tiny head shaking.
There's a childlike joy about him.

Why do we stop playing in puddles when we grow up?

And where does our wonder and curiosity go?

When the sun becomes too much,
we stop in the shade.
Another church waits for us.
We hide under the wooden play house
in the sandbox in the park
next to her instead.

We hold a service for ourselves—
piled together in the sand,
reading scriptures scribbled down
on cotton paper in rainbow pens.
We catch our breath, and eventually,
our makeshift congregation disperses.
Some go over to flower bushes.
Others, to a cafe. A sole few stay
and let the sand fall between their toes.

A father and son play
in the sand beneath
the warmth of the day.
Their cheeks are tinted red,
their laughter, loud.
They build a castle,
then another, then they fall.
They share their late lunch
beneath the safety of a tree.

I write letters no one will read.

We're statues in a museum.
I think back to the muses,
the lovers, the veiled women.

Who will have their heart broken by them today?

The church bells ring
and I'm pulled from my thoughts.
I leave the letters in the bottom of my bag
and rest my hand. There's no point in
wasting words anymore.

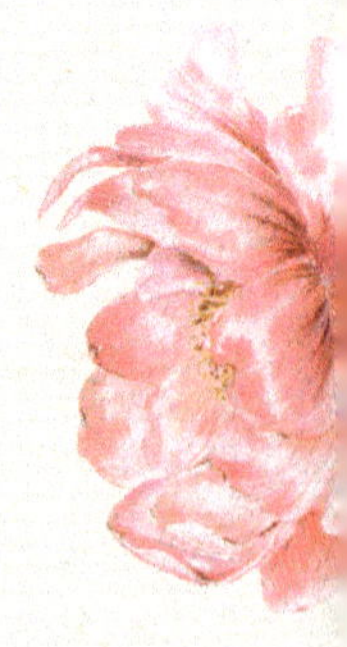

Les cloches chantent une chanson
à la fin de leur décompte.
C'est leur maison, leur paix.
Un corbeau se pose à côté de moi
et penche la tête,
regarde l'église
et puis il me regarde.

Où est votre paradis ?

Il est à un océan de distance.
Un pays entre nos lits.
Alors, ce n'est qu'un fuseau horaire.
Un étage.
Deux portes.
Au lit.
Disparu.

THE BELLS SING A SONG
AT THE END OF THEIR COUNT.
THIS IS THEIR HOME, THEIR PEACE.
A RAVEN LANDS BESIDE ME
AND COCKS HIS HEAD,
LOOKS AT THE CHURCH,
AND THEN BACK TO ME.

WHERE IS YOUR HEAVEN?

HE IS AN OCEAN AWAY.
A COUNTRY BETWEEN OUR BEDS.
THEN, ONLY A TIME ZONE.
A FLOOR.
TWO DOORS.
IN BED.
GONE.

Heaven is just another circle.

When the silence settles over us again,
it's all too unbearable.
We stand and run to the blacktop.
We play hopscotch and sing schoolyard songs,
giggling, falling over, scraping our knees—
finding the joy of childhood again.

And then,
when all of the rhymes
have been made,
all of the bridges
fallen down,
all of the bubble gum
in one dish,
do we dare to move on.

It's here that we find her,
creeping toward the shade.
A bumble bee.
She's so tiny, so tired.
She's picked up by the soul
with the heart of a fae—
her own wings hidden from us mortals.
Then she's passed to me
as a bit of sugar water is poured
into a palm.
This place has provided us
with sanctuary when we needed it.
The least we can do is
care for its smallest citizen.

She likes our rings.
Every time we try to put her down
on a petal or leaf in the shadows,
she grips onto our fingers,
refusing to let go.
We let her stay with us
a bit longer, happily
examining emerald and gold.

I name her Rosaline.

The tiniest hearts
tend to beat the strongest.
Shrouded in stalks of lavender
and tall grass, she waits
for the sunshine
to brighten her path
before taking flight.
Resting her wings—
stained glass panels
that shine rainbow in the sun—
she trusts the strangers
that don't pass her by,
souls tied together
with a golden string
strung with pollen.

We've managed to find
the worst bubble tea
in all of France.

At least we have the memory.

Soft fingers run over
cool marble columns
surrounding the garden.
The ghosts here are shy.
They hide in the corners
of the cloisters, watching us,
wondering. Their whistling
blankets the open space,
making it feel less empty.

I find myself alone
and rest on a ledge.
Time takes pity on me
after so many sleepless nights.
I close my eyes.
When they open,
he's sleeping next to me.

My Dear Dante,

It seems as though you've found me again.
Hell was supposed to be a burning inferno of flame,
but it's freezing.
My fingers are speckled with blue and white,
numbing with every step we descend.
Footsteps fall over the record—
music, a memory, and fading fast.
We chose this path—
a group of happy sinners getting tipsy on champagne.

Hundreds of feet below the surface,
we walk through catacombs
and tunnels. Water drips
down stone walls, running
in thin rivers by our feet.
They're tears, shed by the faces
carved into the darkness.
We follow the stream,
praying for a glimpse of light
between bars when we look up.

The tears of the forgotten
meet their end in a room of echoes
and decay. A desk sits in the center,
snow and salt eating away
at its legs and body.
Still, it stands with what little strength
it has left. The snow falls. The ice creeps.
The pens dry up and the papers burn.
My Dear Dante,
is this the poets' circle?

We warm ourselves with alcohol
and fall in love with our fate.

The village is provincial,
the flowers, abundant.
Smooth legs spread out
over shawls laid in the grass.
Rain is on its way.

Time gives himself to us,
walking with us as equals,
slowing when we slow,
racing when we run across the street,
dodging cars and bicycles.
We're playing a dangerous game
of tag on an unfamiliar playground.

He takes out his journal
and spreads the leather binding,
exposing a new page to a new day.
In a new place, he writes what
he will never share.
I don't ask him to.
He can keep his secrets.

Loving you
is incredibly inconvenient.

A ladybug lands on my notebook—

PUTAIN DE TAQUINER.

FUCKING TEASE.

Love and anarchy
are two vastly different states
that are all too often
found tangled in bed together.
How can devotion and chaos
be confused so easily?
How can so few hearts
see the breaking point?
I suppose it's easy when love is blind,
or whichever excuse they're using.
An arrow is sent whirling through
the sky, a path forged
in someone else's mind.
Cupid, what have you done?
To hurt Psyche like this
when she loved you so?
She willingly gave you
full power over her heart—
but power never stays empty
in the grand perspective of dreams.

He loves me,
he loves me not.
I look at the archer
and do my best
to block his blow.

This hall of mirrors betrays me.
Reveals me. Shows every side
of me that even I can't see,
that I don't know yet.
It projects us in a display
of linen dresses and waistcoats,
forget-me-nots scattered in
stitching and sorrowed eyes.
Neither of us will die,
but we both know that
this is our ending.

We never did make it to the cat café.
But we do make it back to the Seine.
Strangers and lovers dance on the edge—
tango, waltz, salsa. I watch them,
not realizing that I'm moving closer.
One man walks up and holds out his hand.

I politely decline.

I think I would rather like to dance again.

So we dance in the garden— my soul sister and I.
And for a moment, we're princesses.

They record us,
and for the first time
in a long time,
I see the little girl
who dreamed of adventure
smile.

I never liked having my picture taken.
Not because of forcing smiles,
worrying about how my dress falls,
or standing still in an ever-moving world,
but because I'm selfish.

I don't want to waste too much time
posing for pictures and retaking them
because a hair is out of place
or because my eyes are closed.

I don't want to be tied down
to one spot forever in a memory.
I want you to remember me as I am
and let that memory grow with me.

I want you to look at me and
think of the time
we stood on the balcony,
overlooking the gardens,
and you saw me with my eyes blissfully shut,
knowing peace, possibly for the first time.

How the lines that spread
from the corners of my eyes
and into my lashes
were water-stricken with laughter
from the heart that found silence—
how loudly that silence resonated
with my breath.

How the wind blew
my curls this way and that, and
I smiled so deeply that every chipped tooth
met the sun, and my mouth
thanked the day in only the way
a lover can thank the night.

How my dress matched the roses
in one moment, and then whirled around my legs
like vines, tumbling through the wildflowers.

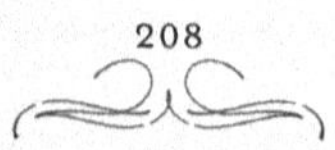

I want you to remember me that way—
easy to pick up and replace
onto any balcony,
on any street,
or garden,
or cobblestone path,
anywhere in the world
on any given day
I wake up with you.

Sunrise over the countryside,
a maze of wildflowers.
His lips taste like honey.
The chickens wake the goats
and the water wakes the wheat.
Tiny towers guard cottages,
ducks guard their ducklings.
A cat meanders by the bees,
busy with their honorable work.
This will be my last moment of rest here.

The ghosts of France
have finally welcomed me.

Faint whistling floats down
with feathers between
window boxes. She braids hair.
I see sunflowers. I think of them,
of first meetings.
His hair was shorter then.
So was mine. Nine are not with us—
scattered across the globe.
My heart breaks a bit more,
not because they're not here,
but because I'm not there.

We find ourselves back in Paris.
Back in a restaurant,
where the waiter somehow
becomes my best friend
even after learning I won't be
eating steak. He asks me three questions.
My answers pick the wine.

Strawberries. Sunrise. The woods.
Seven glasses sit between me
and the man with the dream of *more*.

He buys us all roses.
I press mine in my copy of
The Hunchback of Notre Dame.

There's no space
for ballads in ballrooms.
There's barely any space
to fit us all—
crammed into a row of tables
along a line of bottles.
In time, the pink
will fade from the tips of petals.
I won't be able to recall
what color the labels were.
Their voices will fade from
my memory. But I will
forever remember the taste
of tears chasing wine.

We stay, standing in the lobby.
Do we go up the stairs?
Pile into the elevator?
Just this morning, we were
laughing and wandering the streets,
looking for a post office
to mail an abundance of
letters, wishes, pressed flowers,
and fading promises.
Now we find ourselves silent.
Not even our eyes are brave enough
to speak. Our tongues can't
help form letters. Wishes linger
between stars and reality.
The flowers on my dress
are pressed against the wall.
New promises are made.
We stand awkwardly
in the crowded elevator,
listening to the others
talk about their futures and
how they're going to visit each other.

The only thing we share that night is restlessness.

I join them— the ghosts.
We haunt the hotel lobby.
This time, you're not the first
to wake. When you come downstairs,
your fingers will wonder what to do.

I clasp the hook on my necklace
and turn in my hotel room key.

The Paris morning is quiet
in the moments before the sun rises.
The emptiness of the countryside
has yet to creep back home.
The loneliness waits to pair with us.
One by one, or rather, two by two,
we vanish from the sight of the hotel.
Of the cathedral. Of the Seine. The bookstore.
Beyond the travelers waiting to check their luggage.
Away from the beautiful strangers who will
never know how much they mean to our stories.

I find my gate and wait.
A woman is crying.
She missed her flight.

I hear my group called.
I find my seat.

Tu me manques.

I miss *you*.

Dear Reader,

This book was written
when I had no idea what to say.
These pages were filled
when I was at a constant loss,
trying to find my way
through the streets of a new country
and life. Paths were paved with promises
that had been broken time and time again—
but life is filled with brokenness.

We just need to figure out
how to best take the shattered pieces
and create something new from them.

This adventure was one I never thought
I'd actually go on. When I was little,
whenever someone asked me what I wanted
to do when I grew up, the answer was always:
go to Paris and paint the Eiffel Tower.

Art was my life back then.
I was always sketching and painting,
creating just as much as I was dreaming.
And then I stopped when I found
my first broken promise.
A broken heart. The loss of a family member.
A failed test. Being lied to. Being used.
Big and little life events
that swarmed me until I wasn't even drowning—
I was just laying at the bottom of the ocean floor,
waiting for my lungs to stop working.

Somewhere, before my body stopped sinking,
the little girl that was so hopeful
grew up and stopped dreaming
well before she was ready.

I found her in Norway, standing tall
with her hands on her hips next to a statue,
rolling through the flowers by the fjords,
and talking to the ravens and the reindeer
as though they could understand her
(I like to think they did). And I cried with her.

I held her in my heart and let myself feel
everything I was so scared to accept.
I let her be a little girl again and discover
the child-like wonder of life through adult eyes.
I painted— for myself instead of a grade—
for the first time in years. And I laughed with
an open heart and promised her that
from that moment on, the dreams she had
would come true. That the promises I made
to myself when I was younger
would no longer be broken.

This trip was for her.
As soon as I found out that my favorite
Tennessee Sunflowers were going to France,
I made sure my passport wasn't expired
and began to pile away money in a jar.
I got a new journal and pens, and counted
the days until I could take her there so
she could paint and sing and discover.

The months leading up to the trip were
difficult, to say the least. I became very sick
and wasn't sure I would be able to go.
My body, mind, and heart were at their weakest.
But I needed to make sure that I would be okay—
at least for this one week. At least for long enough
to paint the tower. That was the ultimate goal.

And I did. While it was hard, I healed through the pain.
I kept finding my way back and forth between
the country and the city, and every place I went,
the little girl who was so hopeful found me
and another version of us from the past.

I found sanctuary, not only in the churches and
bookstores, but in the people I met.
This book was written for every lover, for every love,
that I've ever had. For anyone who had ever
shown me safety and care. For every "right love,
wrong lifetime." Because the idea of a sanctuary
isn't just a place— it's the people you meet
along the way. The promises you make and keep.
It's the security that comes with the darkest moments
of life, but still shine through. And love
doesn't always have to be romantic. It can be

found in chosen family, in best friends, in pages
tucked away on book shelves in twenty
different languages. Your heart is a precious thing.

I hope that, as you read this collection,
you thought about your childhood
and the promises you made to yourself
that you haven't been able to keep.
And I hope you pick one, and that one day,
you're able to look back to a past version
of yourself and smile, knowing that the promise
was kept, and that you're able to find sanctuary
in the hearts of those that beat like yours.

       With every speck of stardust,

Chère France,

Tu étais un beau rêve
dont je pensais qu'il ne partirait jamais
de ma chambre ou mes minuits.
Tu étais les taches de rouge à lèvres sur les lettres
et des brins de perles éparpillés
sur les nœuds de satin et les gants de dentelle.
Tu étais le fantasme
de chaque petite fille entre le désir
d'être princesse et celui d'être peintre.

Tu étais et tu es toujours un trésor.

Mais surtout,
tu étais une promesse que je n'aurais jamais
cru pouvoir tenir. Mais j'étais là,
à te rencontrer pour la première fois après
tant d'années
en essayant d'oublier.

Je suis venue vers toi quand j'avais
le plus besoin de toi.
Quand j'avais besoin de guérir, de souffrir, de tomber
amoureuse des gens de mon passé,
de mon présent et de mon futur. Tes rues
m'ont guidée vers des fleuristes

et des structures sacrées. Vers des cloîtres,
des palais et des grottes au fond des profondeurs.

Je ne pense pas te revoir un jour.

Tu étais l'amour d'un moment.

Mais je sais que ça va
parce que tant d'autres viendront à toi
et trouveront la sécurité, l'abri et la guérison -
tout comme je l'ai fait.

Merci de m'avoir laissée tomber amoureuse du
chagrin d'amour.

Merci de m'avoir laissée tomber et me relever.

Merci d'avoir réalisé le rêve d'une petite fille.

Avec chaque grain de poussière d'étoile,
    Freydis

Dear France,

You were a beautiful dream
that I thought would never leave
my bedroom or my midnights.
You were the lipstick stains on letters
and strands of pearls strewn across
satin hair bows and lace gloves.
You were the fantasy that
every little girl has in between
wanting to be a princess and a painter.

You were, and still are, a treasure.

But most importantly,
you were a promise I never thought
I could keep. And yet there I was,
meeting you after so many years
of trying to forget.

I came to you when I needed you most.
When I needed to heal, to hurt, to fall
in love with people from my past,
present, and future. Your streets
guided me to flower shops
and sacred structures. To cloisters
and palaces and caves, deep below.

I don't think I'll ever meet you again.

You were a one-time love.

But I know that that's okay,
because so many others will come to you
and find safety and shelter and healing—
just as I did.

Thank you for letting me fall in love with heartbreak.

Thank you for letting me fall and catch myself.

Thank you for making a little girl's dream come true.

With every speck of stardust,
    Freydis

Hello, wildflowers—

This is a place for you to write your own letters to France— be them from dreams or travel. Fill these pages with your thoughts, doodles, anything you'd like that's brought forth by this country's kiss.

I hope that, one day, you get to see her lights, midnights, and dreams.

Your Letters
to France

ACKNOWLEDGEMENTS

To every soul who held my heart without hurting it
in reaction to the burden of the weight it carried—

To every "right love, wrong lifetime," who, to this day,
still exist in my story as friends—

To every pair of eyes I found safety and shelter in
through every storm—

To every hand that tangled their fingers with mine
as we raced through the rain—

To every pair of lips that shared laughter with me
on cold midnights—

To every shaky breath that found its way
between my confessions and yours—

To the man with the blue eyes—

To my Sunflowers—

To Rachel and Laura and Cheyanne—

To the wildflowers, lovers, and dreamers—

and to *you*—

thank you.

To my younger self—

thank you for not giving up on me,
even when I gave up on you.

About the Author

The works of author and artist Freydis Lova balance the sorrow and ecstasy of life, revealing the myriad of nuances surrounding the human condition and what it means to be alive.

Forever inspired by nature, fantasy, and folklore, Lova composes collections of poetry and prose that take on a dreamscape tone while remaining true to life and its purest emotions.

Lova has earned five degrees in higher education, and has an extensive background in the English language arts. She is an accomplished editor, writer, and lifelong learner— ever fascinated by this world and the languages that connect us.

She is currently based in the American Northeast, spending as much time as she can at the edge of the forest with the wildflowers and wildlife.

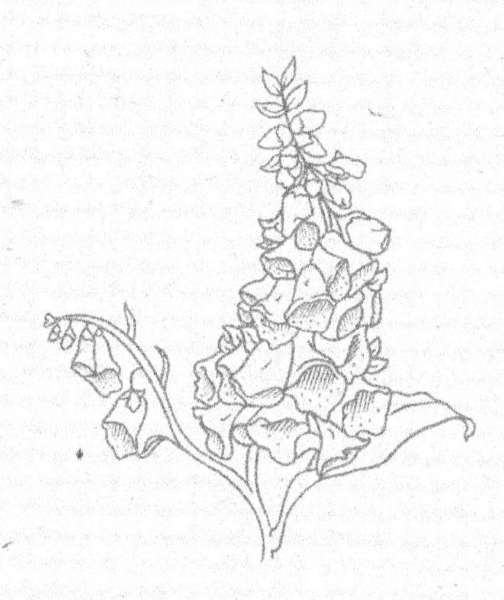